Remote Collaboration with Virtual Reality

A New Wave of Business Integration

Table of Contents

Chapter 1. Introduction

In this ambitious Special Report, we venture boldly into the fusion of technology and teamwork, presenting an insightful glance at Remote Collaboration with Virtual Reality: A New Wave of Business Integration. Simplifying the technical jargon while nurturing the essence of novelty, we've designed an accessible narrative that demystifies how virtual reality is reinventing the workspace. No prior tech understanding needed, we promise! Unearthing opportunities, unveiling challenges, and underscoring efficiencies, our report gently ushers you into a future where distance is rendered irrelevant by advances in virtual reality. Step into this exciting new era of business integration with us! We guarantee, after diving into this stunning exploration, you'll be riveted to the edge of transformative breakthroughs in remote collaboration.

Chapter 2. The Dawn of a New Era: Remote Collaboration Meets Virtual Reality

Technological strides have paved the avenue towards a daringly innovative model of integration, where remote collaboration weds virtual reality (VR). This powerful alliance engenders a stimulating environment conducive to enhanced teamwork, optimal productivity, and resilient business continuity, especially in the face of the unexpected, such as the 2020 pandemic.

2.1. Encountering Virtual Reality

Virtual Reality (VR) had its beginnings in the realms of gaming and entertainment. The technology's primary objective was to move users from their literal surroundings, immersing them in an utterly different, often fantastical, virtual environment. As the technology matured, the applications of VR expanded, venturing into groundbreaking domains, including remote collaboration and workspace productivity. Today, VR is no longer just about escapism; it's about shaping a new dimension of reality in which business takes place.

2.2. The Facets of Remote Collaboration in VR

Experiencing remote collaboration through VR is akin to stepping into a futuristic realm where geographical dispersion is no longer an impediment. Team members equipped with VR headsets can share a virtual workspace, interacting in a manner that closely mimics physical presence. A scenario that typically transpires would include avatars representing team members, convening in a meeting room, engaging in discussions, brainstorming sessions, or collaborative design endeavours.

Shall we delve into VR's impact on various professional arenas?

Product Development: VR's immersive aspect allows architects, engineers, designers, and other creative professionals to construct, visualize, and interact with their projects in a three-dimensional environment. This sort of real-time collaboration cuts back on time wasted during back-and-forths, and fosters more fruitful brainstorming sessions.

Training and Education: These areas have also hugely benefited from VR's ability to generate realistic simulations. High-risk industries like aerospace, healthcare and heavy machinery can provide immersive training environments that mimic real-life situations minus the risk. Similarly, educators can employ VR to facilitate virtual field trips, further enhancing learning experiences.

Conferencing: Scheduling virtual meetings is nothing novel; however, VR intensifies the experience to rivetingly realistic extents. Unlike traditional video conferencing, VR enables participants to express body language, offering nuances of communication lost in emails, phone calls or even video chats. This form of virtual meeting can qualitatively enhance collaboration.

2.3. The Alluring Advantages of VR Collaboration

A significant novelty conferred by VR technology upon the business realm is the capability of creating interactive, three-dimensional virtual workspaces. Generating a sense of togetherness, these virtual environments subvert the "out of sight, out of mind" mentality.

Colleagues feel seen, heard, and engaged, even when operating from remote corners of the globe.

Work-from-anywhere policies are gaining in popularity, and VR reinforces these strategies, offering an inventive solution to combat loneliness, isolation, and disengagement that some remote workers may experience. Workplace flexibility thus need not sacrifice team spirit or camaraderie.

VR collaborations have a distinct edge in facilitating effective training and mentorship programs, cementing the concept of accelerated learning. VR can mimic complex, real-world scenarios in a secure, controlled environment allowing employees to learn and make mistakes without real-life repercussions. The resultant increase in confidence and proficiency is a considerable asset in fast-paced industries where comprehensive training is a prerequisite.

2.4. Challenges Facing VR in Remote Collaboration

Like all pioneers, VR technology in remote collaboration is not exempt from challenges. The cost of robust VR hardware may deter small-to-medium businesses. Additionally, there's the potential alienation of employees uncomfortable with such a technologically intense mode of interaction. Usability issues, addressing VR sickness, privacy preservation, and data protection are other wrinkles requiring ironing.

2.5. The Ongoing Evolution of VR Technology

Despite challenges, the prognosis for VR technology in remote collaboration shines promisingly optimistic. The continual evolution of VR capabilities, coupled with the decreasing cost of hardware, signals accessibility to a more extensive business bracket. Anticipated advancements extend to the incorporation of AI, making VR environments increasingly immersive and intelligent.

2.6. Conclusion

With current strides in VR technology, the dawn of a new era in remote collaboration is here. A day where technological and human elements amalgamate, creating a synergistic blend, fostering creativity, camaraderie, flexibility and productivity in the workspace. The integration of VR into remote collaboration is more than trend; it's a transformative shift in the modus operandi of businesses, propelling us into a digitally-augmented future.

Chapter 3. Understanding Virtual Reality: An In-Depth Technical Guide

It's the dawn of a new era, one where digital landscapes stretch over the horizon and challenge our perception of distance and space. Virtual reality (VR) is at the helm of this revolutionary shift, creating a conduit for dynamic, engaging, and interactive remote collaboration. But what Is VR? How does it function? Where does it find its roots? Read, absorb and unravel this revolutionary technology with us.

3.1. Embracing the Concept of Virtual Reality

Virtual reality is an immersive digital simulation of an environment, creating an 'almost real' or 'beyond real' scenario for the user. It invokes and manipulates our sense of sight, sound, and sometimes touch, convincingly enough to transport us into a different dimension or world. The powerful manipulation of these senses gives VR the power to alter our perceptions of reality and redefine our interactions within it.

3.2. The Genesis of Virtual Reality

Back in 1968, Ivan Sutherland and his student Bob Sproull developed The Sword of Damocles, which is often accredited as the first head-mounted display. However, it was only in the 1980s that the term "Virtual Reality" was coined by Jaron Lanier, a computer philosopher. Lanier's company, VPL Research, developed a range of VR gear like the DataGlove and the EyePhone. Over the years, the evolution of VR technology has been driven by not just gaming, but also fields like medicine, architecture, the military, and of course, business.

3.3. The Building Blocks: Hardware and Software

How does a user engage with VR? The basic hardware elements include a Head-Mounted Display (HMD) and input devices such as treadmills, bodysuits, gloves, or handheld controllers. The HMDs or goggles create the visual illusion, while the input devices track and interpret the user's physical actions and replicate them in the digital world.

On the software side, VR systems can originate in a range of technologies, such as C++, Java, or Python. Game engines like Unity and Unreal Engine have been crucial to the development of VR environments, offering libraries full of physics simulations, AI, and graphics rendering amongst other tools.

3.4. Making Sense of Virtual Spaces

Immersive virtual environments rely on generating realistic sensory feedback, prompting users to suspend their disbelief and immerse themselves within the simulation. This is achieved primarily by engaging three senses: vision, hearing, and touch.

1. **Vision**: Advanced stereoscopic displays generate an illusion of depth. Each eye receives slightly different images, replicating our binocular vision and giving the sense of a three-dimensional world.

2. **Hearing**: 3D audio effects simulate sounds from different directions and distances and establish a realistic aural ambience.

3. **Touch**: Haptic feedback recreates the sense of touch by applying

forces, vibrations, or motions. This is usually executed through devices like gloves or suits.

3.5. The Mechanics: From Motion Tracking to Rendering

The essence of an immersive VR experience lies in two vital components: motion tracking and rendering.

1. **Motion Tracking**: Motion tracking collects real-time information about the user's physical movement and inputs it into the VR system. The three common types include mechanical tracking, optical tracking, and inertial tracking. Each has its benefits and shortcomings, revolving around accuracy, speed, scalability, and cost-effectiveness.

2. **Rendering**: The VR software processes the user's position and actions collected via motion tracking and translates these into adjustments in the virtual scene. The system needs to maintain extremely low latency to ensure that the users' perceived visuals are in sync with their movements, thereby avoiding a break in immersion or causing motion sickness.

3.6. The Inspirational Influence of VR in Business

As businesses overcome geographical barriers and embrace remote work models, VR brings an enhanced collaborative experience. Companies invest in VR to augment training programs, visualize data, and break down complex problems, reshaping the concept of teamwork and productivity. With VR, we simulate the camaraderie of an office, the intensity of a workshop, or the brilliance of a brainstorming session, all from one's living room.

Even as we unravel the complexities of VR, the most exciting aspect is perhaps still ahead of us: What happens when we bring VR, AR, and Mixed Reality together? Called cross reality or XR, this is yet another dimension of VR that holds considerable potential for remote collaboration.

With the continual evolution of technologies like 5G and edge computing, VR's potential in business is dramatic, drawing us towards the thought-provoking question – Are we standing at the curve of the next big digital wave? As we delve deeper and understand these realities better, the journey to answer this question forms a thrilling exploration in itself.

Chapter 4. Driving Forces Behind the Shift Towards VW Collaboration

Large-scale change is rarely triggered by a single factor. Instead, it's a dynamic interplay of many elements that work in unison, each contributing in its unique way. As we delve into the driving forces behind the shift towards Virtual Workspace (VW) Collaboration, it's critical to examine these disparate elements in detail.

4.1. The Advancement of Technology

The most immediate and evident cause of this movement is the staggering advancement of technology. Significant leaps in Internet speeds, software sophistication, and hardware capabilities have provided the necessary infrastructure for Virtual Reality (VR) to flourish.

In the realm of VR, the evolution of headsets from cumbersome, tethered devices to sleek, wireless tools, boasting of super-rich graphical displays, high refresh rates, and accurate motion-tracking capabilities, have significantly propelled VR adoption. Furthermore, new and robust software engines are being designed to support the complex logistical aspects of VW Collaboration, enabling interaction and movement in shared virtual spaces.

Additionally, machine learning and AI integration have significantly enhanced the VR experience. AI-driven VR can offer automated, personalized experiences, analyzing and adapting to user behavior, thus providing a more immersive, responsive environment.

4.2. The Influence of the Pandemic

Another significant driving force has been the COVID-19 pandemic and the subsequent global restructuring of workspaces. With remote work, lockdowns, and social distancing becoming the 'new normal,' businesses had to adapt or risk being left behind. Companies quickly saw the potential of VW Collaboration to facilitate remote teamwork without sacrificing productivity or interpersonal connection.

4.3. Improved Collaboration and Communication

VW Collaboration allows for a level of collaboration hitherto unseen in other remote working tools. Instead of staring at flat powerpoint slides during a meeting, imagine being able to walk around a holographic model of the project being discussed, inspecting it from all sides as you converse with your colleagues.

Moreover, non-verbal cues are vital in communication. Video conferencing tools fall short in transmitting these subtle signals. However, VR technology can recreate these cues, mirroring body language and facial expressions in the virtual space, enriching the overall communication experience.

4.4. Access to a Global Talent Pool

Adoption of VW Collaboration removes geographical barriers, allowing companies to hire the best talent without the need for relocation. It facilitates a globalized work model where teams spread across different time zones can work together as if they're in the same room.

What's more, inclusion and diversity can be amplified in these digital spaces. With VR, you can design inclusive interfaces, making your workspace accessible to people with various abilities, promoting a truly diverse and equitable environment.

4.5. Environmental Benefits

The long-term environmental benefits of remote work and minimized travel are becoming increasingly recognized. With VW Collaboration, it's feasible to reduce carbon footprint significantly since the need for commuting is eliminated, contributing to the global fight against climate change.

4.6. Cost-Savings and Economic Efficiency

VW Collaboration can lead to substantial cost savings. Expenses related to travel, office spaces, and utilities can be significantly reduced or eliminated. Economic efficiency is also improved as time saved from commuting and increased productivity from improved work-life balance add to overall business output.

These driving forces are acting synergistically to propel us towards a future dominated by VW Collaboration. As we continue exploring this fascinating topic, we'll probe more into how these elements affect different facets of our work lives and society at large, leading to a profound change in our perception of workspace and collaboration.

Chapter 5. The Way We Work: The Dramatic Shift in Business Operations

Over the past decade, digital innovation has triggered a seismic shift in how business operations are carried out. Meanwhile, a tide of external factors – from socio-political changes to unanticipated global events like the recent pandemic – have further emphasized the need for operational flexibility. Amidst this cumulative upheaval, Virtual Reality (VR) stands at the forefront, primed to revolutionize the way we collaborate and conduct business.

5.1. The Advent of Remote Work

In the wake of technological advances and changing business paradigms, remote work emerged as an alternative, if not preferred, mode of operation for many organizations. This shift began subtlety, often construed as a flexible bonus for employees seeking to balance their personal and professional commitments. However, as technological competence improved and companies started to understand the financial and logistical advantages, remote work started becoming the norm rather than the exception. This transition was undoubtedly accelerated by the global pandemic that mandated remote work as a critical safety and survival strategy.

Major technology companies like Twitter and Square have announced plans to make work-from-home a permanent feature. A considerable portion of organizations are expected to follow suit due to the evident advantages, such as reduced operational costs and increased employee satisfaction. However, with this comes the challenge of maintaining organizational coherence and effective collaboration in a dispersed workforce; a challenge that VR promises to address.

5.2. Virtual Reality: An Emerging Paradigm

VR, in its most straightforward definition, is a simulated experience that can be similar to or completely different from the real world. With VR headsets and responsive components, individuals plunge into immersive environments, capable of interacting with their surroundings in real time.

In the business word, VR transposes an in-person meeting or conferencing environment into the digital realm. Oculus, the VR division of Facebook (now Meta), has been developing VR-based meeting environments where the physical distance between team members is irrelevant. Meanwhile, apps like 'Spatial' allow individuals to join 'holographic' workspaces from smartphones or PCs, with or without VR gears, making business collaboration more effective and engaging.

5.3. Work Collaboration Through Virtual Reality

In a remote work setup, the conventional video conferencing platforms have served as an immediate solution for business communication. However, they invariably lack the 'in-person' experience that fosters effective collaboration and impromptu brainstorming sessions.

Enter VR – offering a digital space that almost replicates the vibrancy of a physical workspace. With a VR headset, employees can navigate through virtual office environments, participate in meetings with avatars representing their colleagues, and even visualize and manipulate 3D models or charts in a shared digital space, mirroring the nuanced dynamics of a physical team interaction.

5.4. Leveraging VR in Different Business Aspects

The scalability and applicability of VR extend beyond facilitating meetings or collaborations. In training and onboarding new employees, VR can provide a hands-on and engaging experience, which has been proven to be more effective than conventional methods. In sensitive occupations like healthcare or manufacturing, VR-based training can simulate exact working scenarios, giving room for learning through mistakes without consequential risks.

In customer engagement, VR offers potential for immersive product demonstrations and experiences, which could ultimately influence buying decisions. Companies like IKEA and BMW already harness VR to provide potential buyers with a realistic feel of their products before purchase.

5.5. The Future of Work with VR

As we look to the future, the incorporation of VR in business processes promises more than a simple shift from physical to virtual. The potential for an augmented workplace where physical and digital spaces coexist opens up many creative and logistical possibilities.

In a globalized world where the next team member might be continents away, VR presents opportunities for remote collaboration without language barriers or geographical borders. Features like real-time language translation and global access ensure that an organization can operate seamlessly irrespective of the physical location of its personnel.

Despite its benefits, the use of VR in businesses is not without its challenges. Seamless and practical implementation will require overcoming obstacles such as the high cost of VR gears, the need for high-speed internet for a lag-free experience, and health concerns related to prolonged use of VR devices.

Nevertheless, as the technology matures and becomes more accessible, VR's adoption is set to increase, becoming a cornerstone in the future of work as we know it. As we navigate this transformative moment in history, the intertwining paths of technology and teamwork promise a fascinating journey ahead.

The key to a successful transition would be balancing technical innovation with the nuanced aspects of human collaboration. As we ride this dramatic shift in business operations, VR does not replace the office, but reinvents it, providing flexible, collaborative spaces where we can continue to innovate and create even while apart.

Chapter 6. Case Studies: Real-World Examples of VR-Centric Workspaces

Amid a wave of technological change, Virtual Reality (VR) technology is being prominently utilized to create innovative workspaces that defy physical boundaries. In this chapter, we will delve into several examples of how VR technology has been efficiently harnessed to build VR-centric workplaces, pioneering change and pushing limitations.

6.1. Case Example 1: The Architecture of Tomorrow - ARCH Virtual

Arch Virtual, an ambitious VR firm, uses their technology-adeptness to outstrip conventional architectural visualization techniques. Delivering tactile, immersive 3D blueprint experiences, they've changed how architects, engineers, and clients interact with design.

Through VR, floor plans are superseded by interactive, simulated environments. Architects can walk clients through their future homes or offices before even a single brick is laid, while simultaneously allowing real-time amendments. This saves time and money by avoiding detrimental structural changes after construction begins. Furthermore, project stakeholders can convene inside these virtual environments, fostering collaborative decision-making, regardless of their actual locations.

6.2. Case Example 2: Empowering Education - Immersive VR Education

A praiseworthy amalgamation of education and VR is seen in Immersive VR Education. They've discarded traditional teaching confines for interactive, experiential learning in Virtual Classrooms. This application doesn't simply pen to paper; it records, stores, and enables playback of interactive lessons.

The Visual Classroom's usefulness becomes more evident against the backdrop of the global pandemic, where traditional, physical classrooms became health risks. Consequently, numerous academic institutions turned to Immersive VR Education's platform as a sustainable, engaging alternative to face-to-face learning.

6.3. Case Example 3: Revolutionizing Retail - IKEA

IKEA has effectively harnessed VR technology to reimagine experience-driven retail. Through their VR Showroom app, customers can take a virtual tour of their envisioned interiors, choosing from a vast catalogue of furniture items and home accessories. Changes in the arrangement or style can be made in real-time, resulting in an interactive, immersive retail experience.

Their VR initiative further strengthens IKEA's 'try before you buy' philosophy, promoting consumer confidence and satisfaction. Additionally, the virtual store ensures uninterrupted business operations in times of crisis like the COVID-19 pandemic, providing customers with a risk-free method to explore and enjoy IKEA's full product inventory.

6.4. Case Example 4: Optimized Occupational Training - STRIVR

STRIVR, specializing in immersive learning, utilizes VR to train employees through real-time simulations. This approach, a revolution in traditional job training, supports accelerated learning via practical, repetitive tasks in a realistic but risk-free environment.

STRIVR's technology is employed by organizations like Walmart for employee training. Recruits can experience busy Black Friday customer surges from a store's safety, before facing the real-world scenario. STRIVR thus ensures more confident employees, better equipped to handle high-pressure situations.

6.5. Case Example 5: Medical Innovation - Osso VR

Navigating the complex medical world, Osso VR offers a VR-driven surgical training platform. Surgeons can practice procedures in a hyper-realistic virtual operating room, maximizing their skill proficiency before real-life application.

Osso VR enables flight-simulator-like training for surgical practitioners. Moreover, surgeons globally can collaborate, study, and enhance their surgical techniques without geographical limitations, contributing to better patient outcomes.

These real-world examples showcase the remarkable potential and breadth of VR applications. Revolutionizing industries from architecture to medical, VR has proven to be an effective tool for remote collaboration and business integration. Interested sectors thus need to harness its potential to stay competitive in the ongoing digital revolution.

In the next chapter, we will explore further novel developments within the VR industry and make a conscious attempt to understand how businesses globally can adopt and adapt to this breathtaking technology.

Chapter 7. Tools of the Trade: An Overview of Leading VR Technologies

Virtual reality (VR) devices have become central to remote collaboration, providing expansive environments where users can interact and contribute to shared ideas. Below, we delve into a comprehensive survey of VR technologies facilitating remote collaboration today.

7.1. Hardware Solutions

Virtual reality began its journey with hardware, and several manufacturers have led the way in VR innovation. Let's explore the key players:

1. **Oculus Rift S and Oculus Quest 2:** Owned by Facebook (Meta Platforms Inc.), Oculus offers two flagship devices. The Rift S, connected to a PC, delivers high-quality VR experiences. The Quest 2, a standalone device, is known for its convenience – no PC connection is required. Both devices feature positional tracking and provide outstanding VR experiences.

2. **HTC Vive and Vive Pro:** HTC Corp's offerings are often considered top-notch for business applications. Known for their precision tracking, these headsets are tethered to a PC and thus deliver high-end VR performance.

3. **Valve Index:** Created by Valve, the company behind the Steam game store, the Index caters to high-end users with features like high frame rates and fidelity.

4. **HP Reverb G2:** Co-developed with Valve and Microsoft, this headset stands out for its high resolution, providing a crisp and

immersive VR experience.

7.2. Software Platforms

Virtual reality hardware provides the groundwork, but it's the software that brings the virtual world to life. Let's examine some leading platforms that enable remote collaboration:

- **Bigscreen VR:** Popular for virtual meetings, Bigscreen VR enables users to share their desktops in a 3D virtual environment. It even allows for virtual movie nights!

- **Mozilla Hubs:** An open-source option, this platform lets users create and share virtual spaces in their browser, which can be accessed by others via a web link.

- **Rec Room:** This social VR platform lets users create and participate in events, games, and other virtual social experiences.

- **AltspaceVR:** Another social VR platform, AltspaceVR provides virtual spaces that can be personalized for meetings, events, or casual get-togethers.

- **Spatial:** Primarily for collaboration, this platform merges augmented and virtual reality, allowing participants to join either from a VR headset or a smartphone.

7.3. Project Collaboration Tools

What good is a virtual room if you can't work on projects together? Advanced VR tools make project collaboration a breeze, irrespective of your geographic location.

- **MasterpieceVR:** A creative tool that lets multiple users work together in 3D modelling, animation, and painting tasks.

- **Gravity Sketch:** This tool specializes in 3D design, enabling users to collaborate in real-time for product design, architecture, and several other applications.

- **Tilt Brush:** Created by Google, Tilt Brush is an innovative tool that lets users paint in 3D space.

- **Sketchbox:** This tool provides a shared space for teams to brainstorm, design, prototype, and review 3D models. It's particularly useful in UX and industrial design.

7.4. Training and Development Tools

Virtual reality isn't just for meetings and brainstorming sessions; it can also be a valuable tool for training and development. Simulation training is becoming increasingly popular, especially in technical fields. Here are some platforms that make use of VR for immersive learning:

- **STRIVR:** This tool uses VR to train employees in various industries, from corporate workplaces to sports fields and everything in between.

- **VIRTRA:** VIRTRA specializes in law enforcement and military training, providing hyper-realistic scenarios to prepare officers for high-stress situations.

- **Osso VR:** This platform applies VR to surgical training, providing a virtual space to learn and practice surgical techniques without risk.

7.5. Troubleshooting and Maintenance

Despite the best efforts of technology, issues can arise, and users may need help troubleshooting their VR hardware and software. Thankfully, several services help users tackle their problems:

- **VRTK (Virtual Reality Toolkit):** An open-source tool that offers solutions to many VR development challenges, including testing and debugging.

- **VRChat SDK:** This tool allows users to create and publish their own VR experiences and includes features for troubleshooting these experiences.

The landscape of VR technologies is wide and rapidly evolving, with continuous innovation opening up exciting avenues for remote collaboration. As we conclude this exploration, we reflect on one prudent thought: the power of VR lies not just in the headset you're using, but in the imaginative ways it can enhance your workflow, improve team interaction, and revitalize business operations. The tools highlighted here have honed and harnessed this power, marking their place in the vanguard of a transformative wave of business integration.

Chapter 8. Overcoming Challenges: Technical, Social, and Psychological Aspects

Distance is no longer a hurdle as technology continues to evolve and adapt, paving the way for remote collaboration. As we tread into the realm of virtual reality (VR), coupled with seamless teamwork, several challenges stare back at us. These could be technical roadblocks, social constraints, or psychological impacts. Understanding these challenges becomes the first step in turning them into opportunities.

8.1. Technical Aspects

Virtual reality technology in the field of remote collaboration is still in its nascent stage. A couple of key technical issues that are faced in this domain include hardware compatibility and the variation in levels of immersion.

1. **Hardware Compatibility:** VR systems often require high-end, top-tier hardware which may not be readily accessible to all users. The wide range of devices available raises compatibility issues. This discrepancy can obstruct smooth communication and hinder collaborative tasks.

2. **Levels of Immersion:** The level of immersion varies based on the VR device's specifications. While some may be equipped to provide a fully immersive experience, others might offer limited features. This disparity can affect the consistency and productivity of remote teams.

The good news is, technology firms are relentlessly working to iron out these kinks. In fact, the advent of cloud-based VR may soon reduce the high hardware requirement, making VR more accessible.

8.2. Social Aspects

While VR promises to transcend traditional collaboration barriers, it also brings social challenges on the table.

1. **Siloes and Exclusivity:** Working in virtual environments can unintentionally create siloes among remote teams. Inevitably, team members with advanced VR capabilities are more active, thus creating a divide.

2. **Technical Divides:** Not everyone is technology-savvy. The gap between those who effortlessly navigate VR and those who struggle can lead to power dynamics and may impact overall team performance.

Fortunately, there are ways to soften these impacts. Encouraging open dialogues, creating an inclusive rather than exclusive environment, and periodic training can go a long way in mitigating these issues.

8.3. Psychological Aspects

A prolonged excursion into the virtual world has psychological implications too.

1. **Perceived Isolation:** Despite being connected virtually, employees may feel isolated without physical interaction. This can lead to psychosocial stress and impact their well-being.

2. **VR Sickness:** VR systems can induce symptoms similar to motion sickness, including nausea and dizziness, a phenomenon aptly termed 'VR sickness'. This could hamper the overall user experience.

Organizations need to be mindful of these psychological aspects.

Regular team building activities, wellness programs, and breaks from VR can help in managing these aspects better.

8.4. Bringing It All Together

Overcoming the challenges presented by remote collaboration using VR might seem daunting. However, acknowledging these challenges is the first step towards reigning them in. Just as any other cutting-edge technology, VR has its own set of roadblocks and limitations. It is important to educate and prepare your team for what lies ahead in this exciting new phase of business integration.

Technology is advancing at an unprecedented pace, and it is up to us to ensure we tap into its potential while mitigating the hurdles that come along. If managed well, the technical, social, and psychological challenges posed by VR can be transformed into pathways that lead us further into this promising future of remote collaboration.

Chapter 9. The Economic Impact: Balancing Costs and Benefits of VR Integration

While integrating virtual reality (VR) into the business processes has implications that reach far beyond the technological sphere, it is the economic impact that holds significant weightage in decision-making. Between the price of VR equipment and the long-term benefits promised by this technology, how businesses negotiate the cost-benefit trade-off determines the scale and speed of its implementation. This chapter delves deep into these economic considerations, exploring the financial complexities associated with VR integration.

9.1. The Initial Investment: Unpacking Costs

Most understandably, the first obstacle encountered by businesses considering VR integration is the initial investment required. This includes the costs of the VR headsets themselves which can range from a few hundred dollars for lower-end options, into thousands for high-quality, enterprise-level devices. Additionally, most VR platforms require supplementary hardware, such as high-performance computers, the price of which can further escalate the initial spendings.

However, this investment doesn't just end at tangible hardware. Dependable software to support VR integration is also crucial. Either purchased outright or accessed via a subscription service, the costs can vary sizably. Furthermore, generating VR content is another significant expenditure. While there is a growing market for third-party VR content, many businesses may require customized content, pushing the costs up further.

On the human resource front, companies must consider the costs for training employees to effectively use VR tools and the ongoing technical support. Lastly, like all machines, VR systems are subject to depreciation over time which must be considered while calculating the overall expenses.

9.2. Efficiency and Cost Savings: The Returns on Investment

Having established the cost structure associated with VR integration, it is essential to investigate the corresponding ROI. First and foremost, VR can lead to impressive efficiency gains. Virtual meetings, for example, save travel time both within and between cities and countries. Teams can suddenly collaborate in real-time, regardless of geographic disparities, eliminating superfluous travel costs and reducing associated time inefficiencies.

Beyond meetings, VR opens doors to immersive, efficient training modules. Employees can learn at their own pace and repeat sessions as needed without constraining trainers' schedules or disturbing regular operations. Retail businesses, for instance, can use VR to simulate customer scenarios, preparing employees for various situations without disrupting ongoing business activities.

Furthermore, VR can conventionally be used to streamline design processes. Virtual prototypes eliminate the need for numerous physical models, saving material costs and providing an opportunity to test products in a wide variety of situations. A Boeing study, for example, found that using VR for design layouts led to a significant reduction in production time.

9.3. Unquantifiable Benefits: The Non-Monetary Returns

While it's tempting to focus only on the tangible costs and quantifiable benefits of VR, the intangibles, albeit harder to measure, are equally important. For example, by implementing VR, a company can portray itself as a tech-forward entity, generating industry buzz and differentiating itself from competitors. This could positively impact the brand image, attracting both business collaborations and talented employees.

Moreover, the ability to collaborate in a shared virtual space despite geographical distance can significantly enhance team cohesion. The immersive nature of VR interaction fosters a sense of presence, essential for evolving remote work. Such social benefits can lead to higher employee satisfaction and retention.

9.4. Forecasting into The Future: The Long-Term Economic Impacts

While it is helpful to evaluate current costs and benefits, VR remains an evolving technology. Digital currencies and the increasing interest in metaverses communicate a shift towards more immersive digital experiences and hint at long-term economic impacts.

Predicting exact costs and benefits is challenging amid rapid technology advancements. Still, it's crucial to remember that initial costs may decrease over time as VR technology becomes more mainstream and affordable. On the other hand, the long-term benefits are likely to increase with improvements in VR's capabilities and more widespread acceptance among consumers.

In conclusion, the economic impacts of VR integration are multifold. With a sizable initial investment, the adoption of VR cannot be lightly undertaken. Yet the potential for cost savings, efficiency improvements, and non-monetary benefits make VR an attractive proposition. Furthermore, with the broader societal shifts towards immersive digital experiences, investing in VR may not just be a question of immediate returns but preparing businesses to thrive in the future. Evaluating these economic impacts requires a careful balance between the quantifiable numbers and the less tangible but equally impactful improvements in business processes and overall industry positioning.

Chapter 10. Looking Ahead: Future Prospects of VR in Business Collaboration

Just a few years ago, the idea of remote teams working together in a shared virtual space was the stuff of science fiction. However, the rapid advancements in Virtual Reality (VR) technology herald an era where this is becoming possible. As we explore the intersection of VR and business collaboration, what becomes evident is that their amalgamation holds immense potential for shaping the future of work.

10.1. The Convergence of Collaboration and Immersion

As the global business landscape continues to morph and adapt to new advancements, the fusion of VR and business collaboration promises to redefine the traditional workspace. This starts with transforming the very notion of 'meeting'.

In a VR world, remote meetings can become immersive experiences rather than one-dimensional interactions. Colleagues could gather around a virtual table, fine-tuning product designs in real time, and discussions could occur in dynamic environments optimized for the task at hand, accentuating creativity and fostering innovation. Research in social VR and avatar-based interaction has shown that these immersive experiences can do much to bridge geographic distances, enhancing the efficacy and creativity of team dynamics.

Emerging trends in VR-enabled meetings including spatial audio, and hand movements tracking capabilities, are making interactions even more lifelike. Imagine being able to import 3D models into a shared

VR space to review designs in unprecedented detail, or to travel to a virtual recreation of a location before deciding to open a new store, all without leaving your office. The opportunities are endless.

10.2. VR and Skill Training

Skill training is another area where VR is making significant inroads. Gone are the days of clunky manuals and monotonous seminars. With VR, immersive, experiential learning is becoming a reality.

Consider a new employee that needs to be trained on an unfamiliar software product. Instead of going through a series of pre-recorded videos, they could learn in a simulated environment, navigating the software in a fully interactive and intuitive manner. This hands-on approach could significantly boost learning outcomes and retention rates, making for a more effective and efficient training process.

Industries far and wide are starting to harness the power of VR technology for training. Sectors ranging from healthcare, where surgeons are trained using realistic simulations, to retail, where new store layout designs are virtually tested–all are reaping the benefits of immersive learning and validation.

10.3. Data Visualization and VR

Data visualization stands to gain enormously from the application of VR technology. Instead of presenting data in static 2D graphics on a screen, imagine exploring data landscapes in VR, where information can be scrutinized from all angles.

A sales team could use VR to navigate through complex customer demographic data to spot trends and outliers. Data could be manipulated, filtered, and analyzed in real time, with colleagues scattered across the globe working synchronously in the same virtual space. This confluence of VR and big data will play a significant role in future business collaborations by enabling an interactive approach to data analytics and optimization.

10.4. Challenges to Overcome

While the potential of VR in business collaboration is undeniable, we'd be remiss not to acknowledge existing challenges. First, the technology is not ubiquitous — the cost and hardware requirements might be prohibitive for some organizations. Second, there are substantial concerns around motion sickness and discomfort related to prolonged VR use. Finally, there are issues around privacy and data security in the virtual sphere, which will require robust solutions.

Despite these obstacles, with advancing technology and modified standards, we can expect these issues to be gradually mitigated, paving the way for a full-fledged acceptance of VR technology in the business world.

10.5. A Not So Distant Future

VR in business collaboration is not a far-off pipe dream. The undercurrents of change are already at work, with companies such as Facebook announcing a full-fledged VR platform for work, 'Facebook Horizon Workrooms', and Microsoft bringing VR capabilities to its collaboration tool, Teams.

Business collaboration is set to transform, fueled by VR's potential to foster immersive, interactive, and efficient communication. As we navigate toward this exciting epoch, it's clear that businesses embracing these advancements will invariably hold a competitive edge in the not-so-distant future.

By harnessing the power of immersion and interactivity, and by overcoming the hurdles that currently exist, VR holds the promise of reshaping the very fabric of teamwork, collaboration, and decision making. When the line between the physical and virtual blurs completely, we will officially be in the age of immersive collaboration, thanks to VR.

Chapter 11. Step-by-Step Guide: Implementing Virtual Reality in Your Business

As we sail into the future of digital integration, a practical grasp of relevant technical advancements, such as the implementation of Virtual Reality (VR) into daily business proceedings, becomes imperative. This guide aims to assist you in navigating the labyrinth of virtual reality and harmonizing it with your enterprise's rhythm.

11.1. The Grasp of Virtual Reality

If we are to harness the potential of VR, comprehending its essence is crucial. Virtual Reality is a 3D, computer-generated environment that can be explored and interacted with by an individual. The person becomes part of this virtual world or is immersed within this environment and can manipulate objects or perform a series of actions. Among all the senses catered to, sight and hearing are currently the prime focus of VR technology.

While technology giants like Oculus Rift, Samsung Gear VR, and Google Cardboard are popular for personal use, VR's potential extends beyond leisure. In business, VR has floodgated possibilities ranging from remote collaboration to training simulations.

11.2. Suiting Up: Procuring the Right Equipment

Before surfing the VR wave, suitable gear, such as a computer, VR headset, and controllers, must be procured. Much like any other technological procurement, this decision hinges on:

1. **Budget:** High-end devices like Oculus Rift or HTC Vive may offer more immersive experiences but also cost more. Google Cardboard and Samsung Gear VR provide budget-friendly alternatives.

2. **Computer specifications:** Devices like Oculus Rift require a powerful computer accompaniment. Ensure your current systems are compatible, or be prepared for additional expenditure on suitable hardware.

3. **Software requirements:** Each VR device thrives with specific software ecosystems. Ensure these align conveniently with your current technology stack.

11.3. Stepping into the Pond: Tinker with Existing Market Solutions

Before plunging into the deep, wading in the shallows is advisable. VR has been incrementally seeping into different spheres of business. Seeing how others have innovated with VR can provide a holistic starting point and sow the seeds of inspiration. Microsoft's SharePoint Spaces, for instance, demonstrates the new dimension added to remote collaboration by VR.

11.4. Stirring the Pot: Identifying Opportunities

VR's forte is its ability to simulate real-world experiences. Identify individual areas in your organization that can benefit from enhanced engagement or immersive training. Whether it's giving a virtual tour of new property in real estate or helping employees get hands-on training in machinery operation, the opportunities are endless.

11.5. Catching the Right Waves: Selecting a VR Development Company

Developing a customized VR solution necessitates professional expertise. When selecting a VR development company, ponder over their understanding of your work culture, business model, and specific requirements. delve into their project portfolios and gauge their versatility of supply diverse industry clients.

11.6. Navigating the Sea: Developing a VR Prototype

A prototype is an early model built to test a concept. This serves as a preliminary visualization of your solution and provides a platform for observing and rectifying real-time systemic issues. A prototype should consist of core features, keep user pathways concise, and prioritize ease of navigation.

11.7. In the Eye of the Storm: Effective Testing

Ensure that your test subjects represent your future user base. This stage plays a prominent role in identifying crashes, hang-ups and navigation issues. It also lets you glean insight from users on how intuitive they find the solution to be. Observing real-time usage can also highlight features you may want to add or discard.

11.8. Catching the Breeze: Launch and Analyze

Once testing is completed, your VR solution is ready for business integration. However, the journey doesn't end there. Regular analysis and updates are crucial for an evolving business. Track metrics like usage hours, engagement rates, or task efficiency to understand the impact of your VR implementation.

11.9. Tackling the Waves: Addressing Potential Challenges

Lastly, prepare for the challenges that could emerge, such as difficulty in acclimatizing to the technology, potential cost overruns due to tech issues, and the chance of low acceptance among employees. To address these, a top-down approach for tech acceptance, regular training, and budget allowances can be highly beneficial.

In conclusion, VR implementation is not just a growing trend, it is an investment in improving your business processes, enhancing employee interaction, and offering better services or products to your clients. Like all other technology adoptions, it requires forethought, planning, and a resilient mindset to utilize it fully. Savvy business owners who recognize the inherent potential can seize this opportunity to ride the new wave of business integration.